Questions and Answers: Physical Science

Forces and Motion

A Question and Answer Book

by Catherine A. Welch

Consultant:
Philip W. Hammer, PhD
Vice President, The Franklin Center
The Franklin Institute Science Museum
Philadelphia, Pennsylvania

Capstone
press

Mankato, Minnesota

Fact Finders is published by Capstone Press,
151 Good Counsel Drive, P.O. Box 669, Mankato, Minnesota 56002.
www.capstonepress.com

Library of Congress Cataloging-in-Publication Data
Welch, Catherine A.
　　Forces and motion: a question and answer book / by Catherine A. Welch.
　　p. cm.—(Fact finders. Questions and answers. Physical science)
　　Summary: "Introduces the connection between force and motion and describes the
effects of air resistance, mass, and gravity"—Provided by publisher.
　　Includes bibliographical references and index.
　　ISBN-13: 978-0-7368-5445-0 (hardcover)
　　ISBN-10: 0-7368-5445-2 (hardcover)
　　ISBN-13: 978-1-4296-0223-5 (softcover pbk.)
　　ISBN-10: 1-4296-0223-6 (softcover pbk.)
　　1. Force and energy—Juvenile literature. 2. Motion—Juvenile literature. I. Title.
II. Series.
QC73.4.W435 2006
531'.6—dc22
　　　　　　　　　　　　　　　　　　　　　　　　　　　　　　　　2005020118

Editorial Credits

Chris Harbo, editor; Juliette Peters, designer; Jo Miller, photo researcher;
　　Scott Thoms, photo editor

Photo Credits

Brand X Pictures, 23
Capstone Press/Gary Sundermeyer, 8; Karon Dubke, 10, 11, 12, 13, 15, 24, 25, 29 (all)
Corbis/Charles O'Rear, 6; James Noble, 1; Lowell Georgia, 9; Mark Cooper, cover; Reuters, 18
Folio, Inc./David R. Frazier, 20; Matthew Borkoski, 26
Getty Images Inc./The Image Bank/Tony Anderson, 22; Photonica/Roberto Mettifogo, 14
The Image Finders/Bachmann, 4
Index Stock Imagery/Bob Winsett, 27
Peter Arnold, Inc./AGE, 5; Deborah Allen, 17
Photo Researchers, Inc./TRL Ltd., 19
Photodisc, 7
UNICORN Stock Photos/Jeff Greenberg, 21; Rob & Ann Simpson, 16

The author thanks Judith Stark, Jacqueline Hoffman, and the staff of the Southbury,
　　Connecticut, library for their assistance in gathering material for this book.

062011
006211R

Table of Contents

Features

What is force?

You whack a hockey puck across the ice and into a net. You ride to the park and climb the monkey bars. Every day you use force to move things. Any time you push or pull something, you use force.

Sometimes, you can see the forces that cause an object to move. A pitcher uses force to throw a baseball. The batter smacks a home run with the swing of a bat.

Crack! A batter uses force to hit a softball into the outfield.

Magnetism is an invisible force that draws steel and iron objects to a magnet.

Other times, you can't see the forces causing motion. You can see pins jump toward a **magnet**. But you can't see the magnetic force that pulls the pins.

Do forces always cause motion?

Forces don't always cause motion. Sometimes forces are in **balance** and objects stay still. If you sit still on a bench, you push down with a force. But the bench does not break and fall down. It pushes back with an equal force. An object only moves when the force acting on it is greater than the object's force.

Fact!

Suspension bridges, like the Golden Gate Bridge in San Francisco, use huge cables and towers to create balancing forces that help the bridge stand.

A basketball player uses enough force to slam-dunk the ball.

Sometimes your force is greater than an object's force because your **mass** is greater. Your mass is greater than a basketball's mass. Your body creates enough force to push yourself and the ball. In seconds, you can lift the ball, jump, and do a layup!

How do you increase speed?

The speed of a moving object increases when force increases. In a kayak, your arms provide the force that moves the boat across a lake. If you paddle faster and increase the force, the boat moves faster.

The speed of a kayak depends on how fast a person can paddle.

A racing speedboat can reach speeds of more than 100 miles (161 kilometers) per hour.

You can increase the force of a boat even more by using a gas-powered engine. A motorboat's engine turns a **propeller** that pushes against the water. The force produced by the engine is greater than the force of a kayaker. The boat's speed increases when the engine makes the propeller blades spin faster.

Why can't I throw a football into outer space?

Gravity stops a football from going into outer space. Gravity is the pulling force between objects with mass. The force of gravity increases as mass increases or as objects get closer. Every object in the universe attracts other objects with this pulling force.

Fact!

You cannot see gravity, but you can feel its force. Stand up and hold your arms out to the sides. In minutes, your arms will feel heavy because gravity is pulling your arms down.

What goes up must come down. Gravity will always pull your football back toward earth.

Objects with a great mass, like earth, have a strong pulling force. On earth, all objects are pulled toward the center of the planet. That's why the football falls to the ground.

How do forces work in a pinball game?

Objects need forces to change direction and speed. A pinball machine uses many forces to change motion. It uses forces to speed up, slow down, stop, and change the direction of the ball.

Play a pinball machine to see how forces change the direction and speed of a ball.

12

The force of a flipper shoots a ball until it hits a bumper. The bumper changes the direction of the ball.

To score points, players must keep the pinball out of the drain. Players use flippers to force the steel ball up the table. The ball moves straight until it hits a bumper. The bumper provides a force that changes the ball's direction. As the ball rolls up the table, the force of gravity causes the ball to lose speed. When the ball rolls back down the table, gravity's pull causes it to gain speed.

Will a marshmallow fall faster than a baseball card?

Yes—but not for the reason you might think. The marshmallow weighs more, but gravity causes all objects to fall at the same speed regardless of weight. Air **resistance** is a force that changes the speed of falling objects.

Air pushes against both the marshmallow and card as they fall. The card's shape makes the card catch more air. So the upward force of air is greater on the card. Without air resistance, the card would fall just as fast as the marshmallow.

Fact!

Skydivers spread out their arms and legs to increase the air resistance on their bodies. Increasing air resistance reduces their speed.

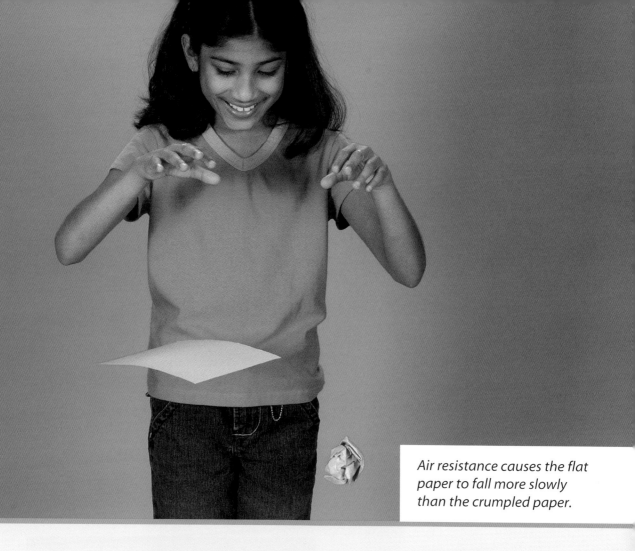

Air resistance causes the flat paper to fall more slowly than the crumpled paper.

Prove this to yourself. Take two pieces of paper that are the same size. Crumple one piece into a ball. Hold both pieces of paper at eye level. Drop them at the same time. The crumpled paper catches less air. It lands on the ground first.

How do birds fly?

To fly, birds need a force greater than gravity's pull downward. Birds take off with the forces created by flapping wings. Some birds run into the wind when taking off. The rush of air under their wings lifts them up.

Fact!

Hummingbirds must keep flapping their wings to stay in the air. They beat their wings about 100 times a second.

A hawk uses the force of rising air currents to glide through the sky.

To stay in the air, birds still use force because gravity keeps pulling them downward. Some birds keep flapping their wings. Others, like hawks, can ride air **currents** caused by warm air rising over cold air. As air rises under the hawk's wide wings, the bird soars upward.

Why do people need seat belts?

All objects have **inertia**. This means an object stays at rest or keeps moving until a force acts on it. When you ride in a car, you are moving at the same speed as the car. When a driver suddenly slams on the brakes, the car skids to a stop. But the riders keep moving forward if they are not wearing seat belts.

Race car drivers use strong safety harnesses to protect themselves during crashes.

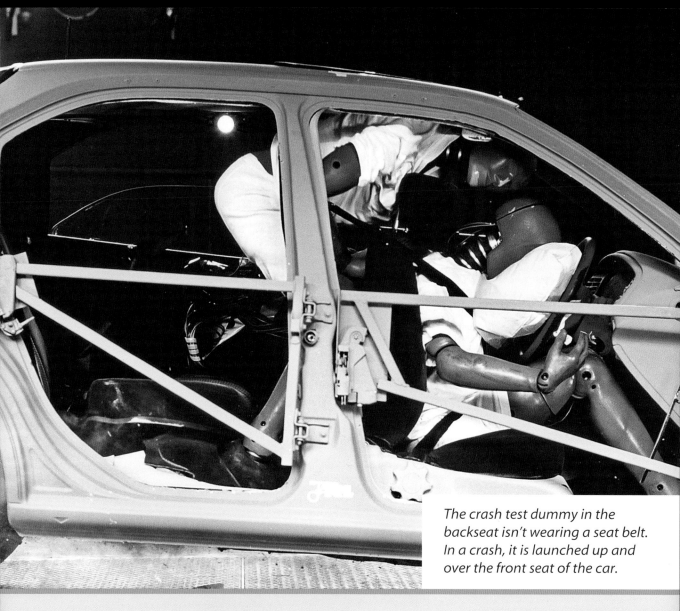

The crash test dummy in the backseat isn't wearing a seat belt. In a crash, it is launched up and over the front seat of the car.

The force of braking acts on a car. But the brakes do not act on the riders in a car. Seat belts stop riders from moving forward and crashing through the windshield.

Why do many highway accidents involve trucks?

Highway driving can be dangerous. Cars, trucks, vans, and motorcycles travel down the road at high speeds. The amount of time it takes these vehicles to stop depends on their size.

Fact!

A car traveling at the speed limit on a dry highway needs about 316 feet (96 meters) to stop. A large truck traveling at the same speed may need about 525 feet (160 meters) to stop.

A huge truck needs more force and more time to stop than a much smaller van.

The force needed to stop a moving truck is greater than the force needed to stop a moving car. Some trucks weigh 20 times more than cars. Sometimes, trucks slam into other vehicles because they take longer distances to stop than cars.

How do trampolines make people bounce?

Sometimes forces can change the shape of objects they push or pull. Some things, like rubber bands and balloons, are **elastic**. The surface of a trampoline is elastic. It stretches when a force acts on it.

Fact!

Soft rubber bumpers make bumper cars safe. During collisions, the rubber dents in to spread out and weaken the force of the crash.

A trampoline pushes you up in the air when its surface snaps back into its original shape.

When you jump on a trampoline, your body pushes down with a force. The surface of the trampoline stretches downward. When the surface snaps back to its original shape, it causes an upward force that launches you into the air. But you aren't headed for the moon. Gravity pulls you back down.

Why does a balloon fly across the room when I let the air out?

Every action has an equal but opposite reaction. Picture an air-filled balloon pinched closed with your fingers. Air causes the balloon to expand because it pushes on the inside walls of the balloon. The walls of the balloon also push against the air. But the air is trapped because the balloon's opening is pinched closed.

Blowing air into a balloon forces the balloon to expand.

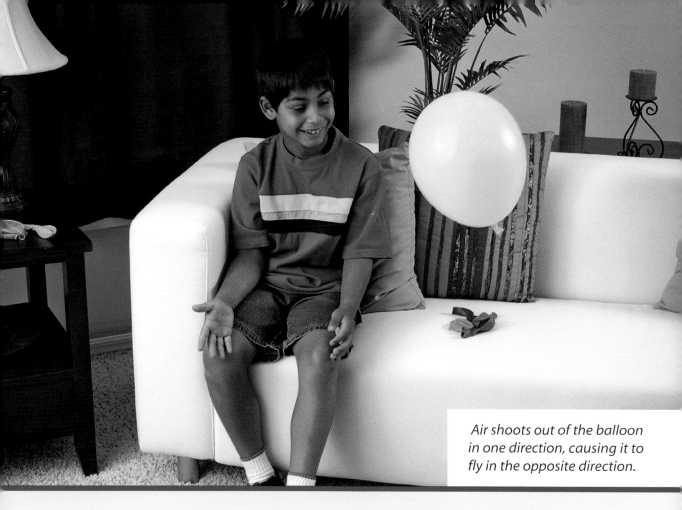

Air shoots out of the balloon in one direction, causing it to fly in the opposite direction.

When you release your fingers, the air can escape. The stretched rubber forces the air out of the balloon. As the air is forced out, it pushes against the balloon with an equal force in the opposite direction. The balloon flies around the room in the opposite direction of the released air.

Why do bicycles have rubber tires?

You are pedaling your bike along a wet trail when, suddenly, a deer leaps in front of you. Good thing you have rubber tires. When you slam on the brakes, the rubber tires grip the pavement to help you stop.

Your bike stops because of **friction**. Friction is a force that slows down moving objects when they rub together. Rough surfaces, like pavement, cause more friction than smooth surfaces, like ice.

Fact!

Smooth surfaces, like ice, reduce friction. A car traveling 60 miles (97 kilometers) per hour needs about 2 miles (3.2 kilometers) to stop on ice.

The friction caused by knobby treads digging into the ground gives tires a good grip.

Mountain bikes have tires with knobby treads. These treads increase the friction between the tire and rough ground. The knobs are able to dig into loose gravel and soft mud. The tire grips better because more of the rubber meets the road.

Fast Facts about Forces and Motion

- A force is a push or a pull on an object.

- Forces are always needed to start objects moving, slow them down, speed them up, or change their direction.

- An object's speed increases when the force acting on the object increases.

- For every action, there is an equal and opposite reaction.

- All objects have inertia. They will stay at rest or keep moving in the same direction until a force acts on them.

- The force of gravity pulls objects toward the center of earth.

- Friction is a force that slows down moving objects.

- Air resistance is a form of friction that happens between air and any object moving through it.

Hands On: Balloon Racer

One of the laws of motion is that for every action there is an equal and opposite reaction. Build a balloon racer to see this law in action.

What You Need

20 feet (6 meters) of string
drinking straw
door with a doorknob
chair
balloon
masking tape

What You Do

1. *Thread one end of the string through the drinking straw.*
2. *Tie one end of the string to a doorknob.*
3. *Pull the string fairly tight and tie the other end to a chair on the opposite side of the room. Push the straw on the string so it is up against the chair.*
4. *Blow up the balloon and pinch the opening shut.*
5. *Tape the balloon to the straw on the string. Be sure the opening of the balloon is pointed toward the chair. Also be sure to keep the balloon's opening pinched shut.*
6. *Let go of the balloon and watch what happens!*

The air shoots from the balloon in one direction, causing a force that pushes the balloon and straw in the opposite direction.

Glossary

balance (BAL-uhnss)—a state when forces are equal

current (KUR-uhnt)—the movement of air or water in a certain direction

elastic (ee-LASS-tik)—having the ability to stretch and return to its original shape

friction (FRIK-shuhn)—a force created when two objects rub together; friction slows down objects.

gravity (GRAV-uh-tee)—a force that pulls objects with mass together; gravity increases as the mass of objects increases or objects get closer; gravity pulls objects down toward the center of earth.

inertia (in-UR-shuh)—an object's state in which the object stays at rest or keeps moving in the same direction until a greater force acts on the object

magnet (MAG-nit)—a piece of metal or ceramic that attracts iron or steel

mass (MASS)—the amount of material in an object

propeller (pruh-PEL-ur)—a set of rotating blades that helps move a boat through water

resistance (ri-ZISS-tuhnss)—a force that opposes or slows the motion of an object; friction is a form of resistance.

Internet Sites

FactHound offers a safe, fun way to find Internet sites related to this book. All of the sites on FactHound have been researched by our staff.

Here's how:
1. Visit *www.facthound.com*
2. Type in this special code **0736854452** for age-appropriate sites. Or enter a search word related to this book for a more general search.
3. Click on the **Fetch It** button.

FactHound will fetch the best sites for you!

Read More

Hewitt, Sally. *Forces and Motion.* Adventures in Science. North Mankato, Minn.: Chrysalis Education, 2003.

Nankivell-Aston, Sally, and Dorothy Jackson. *Science Experiments with Forces.* New York: F. Watts, 2000.

Riley, Peter. *Forces and Motion.* Science Topics. Des Plaines, Ill.: Heinemann, 2000.

Tocci, Salvatore. *Experiments with Motion.* A True Book. New York: Children's Press, 2003.

Index